2016 Hessler Street Fair Poetry Anthology

2016 Hessler Street Fair Poetry Anthology
each poem ©2016 by its individual author

Front cover photo
©2016 by Frankie Metro
facebook.com/frankie.metropolis

Released 7 May 2016
as Crisis Chronicles #85
during The Hessler Street Fair Poetry Contest
hosted by Mac's Backs Books on Coventry
at the Barking Spider in Cleveland, Ohio
hesslerstreetfair.org
macsbacks.com
barkingspidertavern.com

ISBN: 978-1-940996-37-0
1st edition, 2nd printing

The 2016 Hessler Street Fair
happened 21-22 May 2016
11 a.m. to dusk — rain or shine

All proceeds from the sale of this book help support
its publication and The Hessler Street Fair Poetry Contest
sponsored by The Hessler Neighborhood Association

Crisis Chronicles Press
John Burroughs, editor
3431 George Avenue
Parma, Ohio 44134
www.crisischronicles.com
ccpress.blogspot.com
facebook.com/crisischroniclespress

2016 Hessler Street Fair Poetry Anthology Poets
in order of appearance

A.D. Adams
Stephanie Alexander
Michael J. Arcangelini
Jameson Bayles
Dianne Borsenik
Colton Bose
Jeffrey Bowen
Nancy Brady
Steve Brightman
Theresa Göttl Brightman
Christina M. Brooks
Skylark Bruce
William Burkholder
Chad Burrall
John Burroughs
Joann Celleghin
Michael Ceraolo
Shelley Chernin
Charles Cicirella
Lorraine Cipriano
Victor Clevenger
Wanda Morrow Clevenger
Caitlin Blair Cogar
Juliet Cook
A.S. Coomer
Roger Craik
Subhankar Das
Lori Dean
Pamela Dengler
Christine Donofrio
John Dorsey
Kevin Eberhardt
Poetessa Leixyl Kaye Emmerson
Diane Vogel Ferri
Richard Ferris
Francine Flatley
Justyce Foss

Kelle Grace Gaddis
Joshua Gage
Hannah Gates
Christopher Alexander Gellert
Ken Gradomski
Michael Grover
Jennifer Hambrick
Richard Harries
Charles Robert Hice
Veronica Hopkins
Alina Howard
Christine Howey
Dionne D. Hunter
Clarissa Jakobsons
Azriel Johnson
Chuck Joy
Stan Kaufman
Sue Kaufman
Diane Kendig
Kim theBwordpoet
Mindi Kirchner-Greenway
Paul Koniecki
Leonard Kress
Tom Kryss
Lori Ann Kusterbeck
Jill Lange
Phyllis Lee
Lennart Lundh
Susan Mallernee
Marc Mannheimer
Julie Ursem Marchand
Elizabeth Marino
Jonie McIntire
Sarah McIntosh
Frankie Metro
Marisa Moks-Unger
Anne Marie Moore
Laura Moore
Tracie Morell
Leah Mueller
Elliot Nicely

Tanya Pilumeli
Alois Polzer
Tam e. Polzer
Valentina Ranaldi-Adams
Brianna Robinson
Melissa Rose
Damian Rucci
Rikki Santer
Sharon M. Senal
Elizabeth Senn
Aisha Marie Smith
Kevin Frederick Smith
Rob Smith
Steven B. Smith
John Stickney
Katherine Sturniolo
Brian W. Taylor
Jonathan Thorn
Anna Marie Tokarsky
Kerry Trautman
Mary A. Turzillo
D.R. Wagner
Scott Wannberg
Alinda Dickinson Wasner
Laura Grace Weldon
Madison Whitacre
Rosemarie Wilson
Eva Xanthopoulos

Wind
by A.D. Adams

winds flow, grass waves
winds join, swirls begin
clouds darken, rain falls
winds gather, tempest forms
winds twist, earth shreds
village rendered, death dealt
winds fade, child cries
wind gone, world returns

Wolf-Song
by Stephanie Alexander

My coat is long
and keeps me warm,
yet ice crackles
beneath my paws
and clings to my fur.
Wind whips into my face.
I close my eyes in squint.

I am alone on the frozen tundra.

My family has ousted me from their number,
but I am glad because had I stayed I would
have been trampled and humiliated,
not allowed to eat until the rest had fed
and then only leftover scraps.

A litter-mate, my own brother, was alpha.
I, omega.

I am outcast, but life is not so bad.
If I catch a hare or some other small thing
I do not share it.
I find rest in a cave or tree hollow.
I am lonely, but my soul is my own.

This is my existence... for now.

Someday I will find a mate,
start a new pack.
I will be joyous.
I will raise my voice to the heavens.

I will howl.

I Should Fall in Love Again
by Michael J. Arcangelini

Because it has been too long
because I've forgotten what it feels like
because I have curled up too far into myself
because winter is coming and every night grows colder
because too many of my friends are getting married
because I need a date for their weddings
because I can't keep living for myself alone
because I need to care for someone else
because my cat has been dead for four years
because I've forgotten why I swore off love
because I've always been a bit of a masochist
because I've always been a hopeless romantic
because I need a new kind of pain in my life
because I've grown to appreciate my own farts
because I need a reason to exercise and diet
because I need someone to cook for
because I cannot walk on the beach alone anymore
because I have curled up too far into myself
because I've forgotten what it feels like
because it has been too long since I've fallen in love.

Reinventing the Dead
by Michael J. Arcangelini

Sometimes I have the face
but the name is lost or
I'll have a nickname but
reach and scratch for the
birth name with no luck

Other times I have a name
but stumble around my memory
digging to unearth the face
to which it belongs

I am no longer remembering the dead
I am re-creating them,
reinventing them for
my own purposes
drawing out their nobility
accenting their evil
increasing their affection
redefining our relationship
until it meets my current needs
and they are not here
to get in the way
they aren't here to prove me wrong
they can no longer disappoint me,
shame me, best me, please me
they can no longer love me
and it is no longer them
who I love
it is my image of them
assembled from the memories that remain,
the objects, photographs, notes and letters
which carry them with me into
whatever future I have left.

The Engagement
by Jameson Bayles

when you enrapture
a whisper
or an evolving memory
time
becomes your
next of kin

pirouetting
among the synapses of thought
continuance lashes out
a mirrored metronome
out of tune

looking for
a riot to hold onto
I now have seasons that
God
may not
forgive

my vice and virtue
a cracked window pane affianced
sin and grace
a betrothed progenitor
whose unending argument
lodges logic in an illogical
sacrament

how fragrant,
eventually

(eventually)

In a Bar, the Basement, a Microphone, and Poets
by Dianne Borsenik

Ave, ave, cathedral of drink, holy temple of fizz,
bubble and clink, of bourbon, of whiskey,
cognac, rum, tequila, of vodka and XX,
dram, draft, glass, bottle, shot, pint, brew,
every sip a communion sanctioned by dot gov,
Father Bartender blessing me, blessing you,
giving us all another chance to forget
how tomorrow might play out, what our chances
in this crazy game of life might be, and in the corner,
juices pulsing down the throat of the mic, Hpnotiq,
kicking ass, kneecapping the competition, flip,
laughing, unrepentant, irreverent, a literary mojo
more intoxicating than any proof alcohol, more than—

Lesson
by Colton Bose

I have too many dreams
to sleep at the wheel now
I have too much love that
I must express somehow

in life I have learned
even the strongest cry
when they are torn apart
with little reason why

swords and daggers abound
danger is always there
but that is the reason
you should never be scared

when you find yourself lost
with no hope of return
just remember that means
there is something to learn

Wedding Collage
by Jeffrey Bowen

our words are the calls
of a magnificent flock of birds,

bouncing off the canyon walls,

water
as it brightly falls
from a thousand-foot-high cliff,

a smoky, sleepy,
trumpet riff,

temple bells from across the ages,

fingers
that are gently turning pages
in pursuit of ancient art,

as we carefully walk the chambers
of this ever expanding heart.

there are no coincidences,
there are only lightning-like opportunities to see,
with clarity,
illuminated connections,
and sense our roles
as synapses within a larger being.

in addition to the sweetness of the ensuing silence,
there are the added benefits
of drawing strength
directly from the earth,
turning sunshine into gold,
possessions into gifts,

attracting artists, musicians and wild animals like a magnet,
living at the top of the heap by eating from the bottom of the food chain,

routinely scaring off malevolent spirits,
and curing headaches, colds, anxiety and bad dreams,
for those who will let us.

here are sweet roses for you

and red and orange
autumn leaves

and bright yellow dandelions

soft white queen anne's lace

purple cone flowers

and cattails
sea shells
feathers

sand
soil
compost

peppermint leaves
white sage
black coffee

driftwood
beach glass
pebbles

crystals
healing herbs

a snapshot of the sunset
a drawing of the moon
a map of the stars
a dozen poems
a weathered sketch book

a gathering of people who love you
who are gratified by your presence
and your love for each other

the gentle mingling of all that you are

your incredible talents
your open hearts
gentle nature
and generous spirits.

congratulations and best wishes
for safe travels
on this remarkable journey,

play music as much as you possibly can,

read voraciously
and write every day,

spend lots of time outdoors,

find the living creatures that are everywhere
and listen to them,

treat everyone and everything
with kindness,

keep your hearts open
and your minds clear,

listen to your intuition,

to the moon as it tugs at the seas
within your veins,

to the wind in your lungs,

the fire in your hearts,

the earth beneath your feet;

face each day with graciousness
and grace,

and embrace each moment,

as these moments
are all that will ever be.

Dictionary Elles
by Nancy Brady

Lewd, lascivious, licentious, lustful, libertine...
Who found them?
Was it Christy?
Karen?
Or, perhaps, another?
No matter, we learned them
Different words with subtle nuances
All with the same meaning.

We knew them, used them
We were the Dictionary Girls
 Virgins all,
Dateless on Saturday nights.

We believed our teachers,
 The ones who said,
"If you use a word ten times,
The word is yours forever."

And we made them ours,
Lewd, lascivious, licentious, lustful, libertine.
It became our mantra; each having her favorite

Mine, licentious...
 I loved the sound, the feeling of it in my mouth
 Feline, lithe, lean, and smoldering,
 A svelte woman in a skinny black dress.

We're grown now,
 Having lived the lustful life of the mind
 Still Dictionary Girls
...and have become, in turn,
Lewd, lascivious, licentious, lustful libertines
 At times.
But mostly we are just
 Dictionary Girls.

Three Thousand (for Momen)
by Steve Brightman

when the ocean wants you
it doesn't matter how many tears
Puerto Rico will shed for you
the ocean will still take you
it doesn't matter how many tears
flood the Monongahela Valley
the ocean will still take you
three thousand wails

flood the Monongahela Valley
three thousand hits still
three thousand wails
never quite fade away

three thousand hits still
do not forget the skin
never quite fade away
disappearing into the dark
do not forget the skin
Puerto Rico will shed for you
disappearing into the dark
when the ocean wants you

Untying of the Axis
by Theresa Göttl Brightman

After one hundred and one years,
seven blackened days in the tomb—
more than twice as many as Christ spent
behind the stone—
should repay any debts
for crushed stars between dirty fingernails,
should garner a rebirth to angels in gold and white—
not nylon and dust police jackets—
should earn some Lazarus feast.

Instead of an angel-hoisted palanquin,
instead of olive branch parades
and blind men praising the color of the sky,
a helicopter extraction replaces
illuminated ascension,
an ankle-broken body without heavenly raiment,
doubly heavy with the bounds of physical law,
watching every miracle of hell topple the Himalayas
onto goatherds and gardens,
spit from the house-become-cairn
into a bruised and unfiltered version of blue
where the mountain tiger
wraps howls around the perimeters of farmhouses,
while the goddess Kali
dances on Shiva's chest,
crushing the ribcage
of the destroyer himself.

All the cave-dwelling sadhus,
all the yogi-saints generating chakra praise,
failed to appease a goddess hunger,
hunger for bonedust and mountain roots,
hunger for a flour ground from the walls
of towers.

Her face shines dark, the dark translucence
of one hundred and eight thousand

locust wings, the darkness of
twisted grief and the outlines of lightless light,
as she juggles our loosened, cracking globe,
laughing.

The mountains fall
without the Messiah Christ.
The great bull balances
on only one leg
without Ramakrishna.
The Kingdom has come and gone.
Helpless dollars cannot prop up
the snapped legs of fallen children.
Chanting holy holy holy
peace peace peace
shanti shanti shanti
sanctus sanctus sanctus,
but no echo replies.

One Last Conversation
by Christina M. Brooks

I will say it now
so you will remember

That when I arrive at this place,
the edge of memory,
this long corridor of forgetting
before the curtains fall,
let me linger here a while.

Do not push me
or rush me to the final exit.

Let me stand here and smell
the late evening breeze.
Allow me to kneel down
one last time, to feel the brook
ripple thru my outstretched fingers.

Let me listen to the mournful song
of the nightingale.
Let me sit here in the shadows
for just a short while longer.

Morning will come soon enough.
But tonight the sky is clear
and filled with stars
and the moon and I
desire one last conversation.

Neighborhood Poetry
by Skylark Bruce

The high-drama yelling
Of neighbors across the cemetery
Sounds a bit like slam poetry.
The forceful rise and fall,
Pitches circling,
Emotions set on skewer.
Roasted egos carried over granite headstones.
On the other side,
Three gleeful children scamper and shriek,
Making obstacle courses of parked vehicles.
They peer in wonder at the new neighbors,
Speaking big words at each other
Around an unlit fire ring.
They have written poems, too,
Jamai insists.
They have all lived poems,
Whether or not they wrote them down.

Soulful Song
by William Burkholder

And her lute plays the melody of a spring chorus
Plucked in rhythmic meter,
In crescendoed time with the swaying of daffodil,
In the lofty flow of cotton wool,
Drifting on the whims of breezes balmy.

She sings in syncopation to rain's gentle beat,
And rolls in throes of passion,
In the coming of Summer's heat.
Yes, her lute plays the melody of seasons come and gone,
Infinite lyric singing,

Spring's sweet soulful song.

Heavens
by Chad Burrall

We were home just as the light left the sky.

Six unkempt strings skittered on a wall,
where their headstock had rested all day.

"That's a good guitar, I think I can see
the top vibrate from all the way over here."

The next night, his song flew to the stars.

Satellites unravel threads from scraps of night
stretched tight between surrounding trees that
ripped them from greater raiments of rose, faded
to black with such rhinestones sparked random.

N' yet
by John Burroughs

I have no words
I have words
But they have no
They have known
Nothing
They were certain
They knew

They knew
I may as well
Spell it G N U
It would be just as true

I have only words
Who want to know
But have always had trouble
Saying no
Knowing

You and the Wheelchair
by Joann Celleghin

Seeming to float freely
You make circles in your wheelchair
Like a giant lead balloon tethered to the house
Some days its poison seeps in
and pools in your ankles.
Your sock feet pitter-pat the floor
Your hands and grab-it tool reaching all day.
Does the chair have you, or do you have it?
Steel wheels that take you places
(as long as it's home.)
Then, he gets you what you need
and sometimes, even what you want.
One day you'll be running in the sun
with your arms up over your head.
Wheelchair rusting in the rain.

Letter About a Supreme Court Justice's Death
by Michael Ceraolo

Dear America,

The pseudo-compassionate have spoken:
we must not speak ill of the dead man
until a decent interval has passed
(and maybe not even then)

                        But
since he didn't die saving a school full of children
or something equally heroic,
the fact of his death
doesn't change what he was in life
                          And
like his death,
        his life was nothing to celebrate

Purple Tears
by Shelley Chernin

The rain had just begun at my place
when I heard that Prince was dead.
At my place, the rain was clear. I shook
my head, my dear. I shook, shook my head,
shook my booty, stomped my feet,
swayed my hips, hair aswirl, my hips swung my
booty, the beauty of beat
beats the death of the master
of electric beauty. Hot wit U,
I jump jump out of my place,
into Paisley Park. You made me dance,
love of my love. You made me dance.

Rubbing My Eyes
by Charles Cicirella

Rubbing my eyes
I cannot believe I'm dying
But I knew it was only a matter of time

Listening to Ron Sexsmith
There's a new challenge every day
I do my best to deny it all

Holding a microphone like a tomb raider
Digging my cock out of my dirty jeans
Once I go up on the mountain I don't plan on returning

I rubbed my eyes
And you were gone
Gone like bad weather or a silver living hell-bent on the changing seasons

There's nothing to it really
You just claw the words out from behind your irreversible eyes
And somedays I'm 5'2 and other days I'm 5'3

I still remember our first conversation
You said very little
And nothing much has changed now

I said I was dying at the beginning of this poem
I may have exaggerated a wee bit
I have a tendency to do that when I'm bored and seemingly out of options

Shift in Orbit
by Lorraine Cipriano

In the current time melt...
drawing moon to planet
imagination to limitless ideas
cosmic machinery at work
celestial travelers meet up
and compare notes pertaining to
surviving a year in space
some being so bold as to go
untethered in order to float
freely for the briefest moments
orbital dynamics in place
gets them back to their comrades
after dabbling in discoveries
of hidden star clusters
one of them decided to bravely
zoom around the Sun for a bit
a yellow dwarf of spectral type
self-revealing and shining bright
sunglasses on underneath spacesuit
Dolce & Gabbana selfies in space
the only way to document it
solar winds changing the course
never to be seen again

The Day Before My 36th Birthday
by Victor Clevenger

And between bites of a chicken and
cheese quesadilla with black
olives and pickled
peppers,
my four-year-old daughter
says "Asshole."
I keep chewing and ignore her.
"Asshole" she says, tugging my
arm and I nod my head.
She gives one last hard tug at the shoulder and
pulls my head down closer to hers;
my ear is at her lips.
"Poopy Asshole" she says and I swallow.
I pat her on the head with my hand and send her to fetch
her mother.
She leaves the room.
She returns with a warm dishtowel
just recently removed from
the clothes dryer.
I shove the last bite of
the quesadilla shell
through my lips, chew it, swallow it, and wait . . .
"Asshole Poopy Asshole"
I watch her swing the white, but
stained from spilled grape juice
towel from side to side like a marching band's
flag and it twirls fast.
It twirls then falls limp.
"Asshole" she says again and this time
I smack the wooden table top with
both of my hands
like I remember seeing
my own father do so many time before.
My hands make a thud and
I shout
"ENOUGH!"
She shouts something mumbled

and runs from the room crying.
The dishtowel lies alone
on the floor as her mother walks into the
room and says
"Do you always have to be such a goddamn Asshole?"
Standing behind her is
my daughter who wipes her eyes and
grins while she peeks her head
around her mother's right hip.
I smack the table again for good measure
and pick up my milk glass.
I drink it and sit it down;
the milk runs slowly down
the sides from the brim.
My daughter laughs victorious, prances down
the hallway,
and I walk to the stove for a second
helping of dinner.

No Choice
by Wanda Morrow Clevenger

takes no talent
to get here
we phantoms
have no choice in
or out

amounting to more
saying doing parting
with a shred
of grace
that's the money
shot

but no, we are the
robins the wrens
the speckies
plowing
beak first into
the same window pane
over over and again
believing we
can go forever

Almost Breathing
by Caitlin Blair Cogar

You found me underground, a lone embryo
and loved me without reservation
Whispering a language to my soul
that needed no translation

Gasping for truth in a population blind
Fresh eyes, you were a beacon among the rest
Seeing me when I couldn't see myself
All of my trust in house arrest

I lingered on the cruelty of being born
into a world where I can be your ghost
Explain to me this absurdity—
why do we lose what we love the most?

Consumed by arduous apnea,
and lungfuls of former lovers
Each year that passes, a different life
with pieces of me you've recovered

Mending tiny fragments until I am whole,
Bride of Frankenstein
Regaining all that was lost in time
This love made a life so crystalline

After all of the bruises and life's clever scars,
after all of the losses and black-tinted memoirs,
You peel off each layer, breaking down my sheathing
you make me feel like I'm

Almost breathing

Carcass Disposal
by Juliet Cook

I pulled him out of the pen
and laid down next to him
and held him and we were one
spasm after another, for hours.

Shaking and exhausted,
but we couldn't fall asleep.
His damned body kept jerking
in uncontrollable circles,
closer and closer to nothing.

Here's what it boils down to.
Tonight feels like the first night
I've taken the garbage out
unfilled with doggy bags.

A vulture mouth opens the lid,
screams like a demon
for not being given
another heart to eat,
spit out bloody debris.

Indian Staircase
by A.S. Coomer

The hazy blue of distance and memory
stretches out, shifts then expands.
These mountains, leaves of trees,
browning away from newborn green,
just in their verdant infancy then,
still are
now that the years have rolled on
like mildly obstructed water,
and time has molded, kneaded something else
entirely out of what remains of me.

Streaks through the palest tepid blue sky
I have ever seen, jet streams and frenzied,
desperate fever dreams of an end.
A stillness. A pause without ceasing,
sustained suspension, a day off forever.

Dangling my feet over the edge,
shoelaces dancing with hopesick abandon,
I couldn't sit still. Movement brought calm.
Or at least the appearance of such.
Everything (almost) jangled into place.

Walking along the ridgeline,
thinking of jumping into the upturned arms of
sycamores and elms, dogwoods waiting
and watching a little further down
patiently enough
like the little grubby fingers just barely placated,
tugging, wringing, wrenching
at her mother's frail, frayed skirts.
The trust fall for the ages. Here's to you, Gravity,
do what you can't help but do.

I guess it spoke volumes that I never did jump,
though I'm still not sure just exactly what it said.

Apple-Core
by Roger Craik

Alone, and glad at last to be alone,
you're gravelling down an unfamiliar road
edged with goldenrod and pale blue flowers,

and eating the apple you had thought
to pack a few hours earlier.
All your windows are down. All around,

America is breathing
soils and moistures, sunlight
pointing out the silos, dappling

ponds on either side; and once or twice
an easy-naturedness of horses, even a foal,
and cows you think of suddenly as kine,

as on you drive, moving through the hours
as morning bends to afternoon,
as shadows tauten, lengthen by degrees

into a different country called America.
And all the while you sense, beneath the wheel,
the four great tires

rolling you remorselessly away,
toward:
everything, you muse, is yours.

Yes, everything,
everything except, somehow,
the apple-core that you without a care

discarded hours ago
but chanced to notice in your rear view mirror
rolling as if wounded, as if it knew

it was no longer wanted,
but wanted still to be with you,
and tried to catch up with the car.

Spring Song
by Subhankar Das

after a bottle of whiskey
when this world becomes easy
and i can even sing a spring song to you
completely off key

but thank god you are busy
with your friends
and forgot all about the call
you promised

I Am Enough
by Lori Dean

I'm not any of my past experiences.
I'm not any of the outside world.
The doctor can say I have this or that,
But that's not me.
I am enough.

Cut my hair.
Shave my legs.
Strip me of my clothes.
I am enough.

Say goodbye.
Leave me here.
I am enough.

I love you forever.
Now, you can go.
I am enough.

Wash away my makeup.
Take away my career.
I am enough.

No car,
No bike,
Only feet to stand on,
I am enough.

From cradle to grave,
I am enough.

Take away my beauty,
The sway in my hips.
I am enough.

Take away my yoga butt,
My breasts,

The arch in my back.
I am enough.

Take away my long legs,
My elegant arms.
I am enough.

My friends,
My family,
They can choose to go.
But I am still enough.

Acne here,
Acne there,
I am enough.

No tools,
No instruments.
I am enough.

In the light,
In the darkness,
I am enough.

No religion to call my own,
I am enough.

No home,
No shelter,
I am enough.

No baby,
No children of my own,
I am enough.

No books,
No words to describe me,
I am enough.

No money in my pocket,
Debt on my back,

I still am enough.
From nothing to something,
I am enough.

The sun rises.
The moon glows.
I am enough.
Hold me tight and never let go.
I am enough.

Look in the mirror
As the image fades in the fog.
I am enough.

Enough.
I am.

Untitled
by Pamela Dengler

Cleveland's wooden street
Lures me back to the sixties
Hessler Street Fair

Blues, jazz, folk and soul
Tunes wafting past verandas
Hessler Street Music

My very first henna
Makes me feel like a hippie
Hessler Street Fair

White Girl Standing on a Street Corner
by Christine Donofrio

I drive down to the hood and want to shake hands with the locals
I am a fat woman making my way through the world
I have had the door shut in my face and I have been laughed at for being fat sitting at a café
But white is my privilege- and I look at the beautiful exotic lady sitting next to me
I want to tell her my experience and say I understand
But do I really understand
In my upper class neighborhood where I grew up they will call the cops when a black man walks down the street
People are judged for their race and society is aloof
Yet others want to say there is no racism that exists
I stand on the corner and shout my praise
Wake up America from the outside looking in

The Ghosts of Kell Robertson's Chickens
by John Dorsey

here even the wind
has bones

i can hear you laughing

licking the wounds
of imagination

until nothing
feels invisible
not even death.

The Stigmata of Crazy Mark
by John Dorsey

your sleeves rolled up
cigarette dangling from
your lower lip

as blood flows
down your arms
with pride

after a morning spent
banging a chainsaw
against the wind

through burning fields
of savaged oak
through the bones
of a briar patch

you tell your story
at the local fried chicken buffet
without bothering to exhale

oh my gawd
you say

you just need
some fuel
for the fire.

2 a.m.
by Kevin Eberhardt

Walking the fenced in
Parking lot like a lifer
W/out parole listening
to the fluorescent hum
Of electric lights sing a
Cicada song as church
Bells chime for some
Ungodly reason & there
Behind a half closed
Factory 2 & a half men
Engage in a loud debate
I never realized how
Noisy an early morning
Could be unless you
Count the time I was
Stranded in a bar be
Tween last call & a full
Beer & the jukebox
Kept yelling at me to
Take some job & shove
It 'cause I ain't workin'
There no more

Paper Blues
by Poetessa Leixyl Kaye Emmerson

In these azure hours she thinks of how he breathes.
Of how his subtle vapor is tethered to her slight smile.
A mist hangs low beneath this Birch. He tenderly whispers,
"come here", like he always does. The papery bark rustles.
Minute tears go unnoticed by the fragrant air. She is made—
made to wonder, does he want me to rock him like a baby?
Or does he want me to rock him like a hurricane?
He meets her where the moonlight falls on the melody.
She is so unaware of her own dancing desires that
she finds it difficult to run this maze. She is holding herself
in lock step, fanning the fire of expectations—
there is a blooming nirvana in her head and
all the holy ghosts are rolling out of their graves—undead.
In the corner room of her heart Kimbrough's swoon
rhythmically drums up the swelter, the sweat, the sweetness
of all night long long long sex. The gauzy misunderstandings
float dirt and bruises on the precipice of sound, unleashing
perfect disasters and kisses that creep into bed. These shadows
in the night make her think twice about this moment—
this moment that makes her think twice about the
tall trees in Georgia or the Lake Effect Snow, or the
distant weight of his glorious measured words on her
small small small life. The blue mud of love bends and bruises.
Silent kisses curve the fences, leaving poetry
to collect the differences.

The Boneyard
by Diane Vogel Ferri

Lonely tables and chairs suction
clusters of youth around them
as night comes, pulling them in
with brown bottles, tall glasses,
giant screens display frantic
human activity, blinking,
flashing, numbers, talking
mouths with no words,
bodies multiply like mutant cells,
disco music forces itself into
your ears and causes the bodies to bob
like blond-haired engine pistons.
Stalker-looking men tell you
your daughter is beautiful
and you want to take her home
but you can't because she's all
grown up. As the night goes on
you feel older and older,
but the drummer looks at you,
because you still love to dance,
and you know you're not dead yet.

This Is a True Story
by Richard Ferris

She snuck into my bed
in the quiet of the night
fussing with me
caressing me with
soft inspiration

relentlessly whispering
into my ear
until finally I relented
and took her full on

while my wife
complained
on my other side

I rolled with my seducer
writing
and rewriting
this poem.

Folding
by Francine Flatley

Silence falls
upon this house of cards.
A child's
three-wheel bike
rusts
in a long
neglected yard—
grown wild
with brambles
and weeds,
dried up stems
and brittle,
brown leaves.

TV light
flickers
in a musty blue room.
Boxes
line up
in an indifferent mood—
waiting
for someone
to take them away—
as the sun
filters low
through a cracked
window shade.

Black Magic
by Justyce Foss

Black magic sparked between us,
Took me places never mentioned.
One look into your golden eyes,
My body's at attention.
Can feel my blood flow freely,
As my body starts to listen.
Your spirit wrapped around me tight,
I'm at your disposition.
My breathing slowly ceasing,
As my heart is beating faster.
No longer have control of the
Emotions that I'm after.
Hypnotically, you touch me,
Euphoric to my lips.
You run your wand through my hair,
But I can feel you in my hips.
Darkness falls around us,
As I fall into your being.
No lights flicker around us,
Dark shadows what I'm seeing.
I touch for validation,
Wondering who's there.
Want to peel away your mask,
Search for truth,
Not dare.
Who is this thing unknown,
How do I solve this riddle?
These thoughts run through my mind,
While its hands reach for the middle.
Of my heart, in the dark,
Temptation running high.
Quickly switch the lights,
As it turns to say goodbye.
No sign, of whom it may be,
A back that's turned my way,
My feelings are on edge,
My heart is now at bay.

I think about it often,
Who's captured my heart,
It started with one touch,
But it ended in the dark.

For Love
by Kelle Grace Gaddis

I'm for love
Marriage is a lost dream,
ask me how many times I've fallen—
About the collapse
of the middle class,
the income gap,
and the problem with rap being
called, "a poetry for the masses"
We agree, at the end of a shared bottle,
on everything, except you
My non-committal
I want to sentence you
to being alone, but
I'm for love, so I
deliver another acquittal

Lake Erie Winter
—after Donald Revell

by Joshua Gage

It is conceivable that the glass and concrete
curve in such a way, in such a mannered disproportion,
that the whole city becomes a cathedral.
Nothing has changed along these streets you walk.
The grey sky collapses onto grey water, grey horizon.
There are places, doorways and corners, to curl
into like pews to forgive your sober thirst.
Voices you can't trace rise and whip the wind
into wanderlust. You move your feet, convinced
that if you could wrap yourself around the gentle snow
the way these buildings do, you would rot
a little more slowly. Perhaps if you dreamed
the way architecture dreams, you might even heal.
The cold ascends to mock the bones beneath your skin.
and mark the assigned paths of the city. In this retrieved light,
the streets smell of myrrh and old rain. Your feet
attend in blank regard. But you are here for the curves.
Look up. Look at how the buildings close in
lovingly around the snow. Look at the grey sky, the angels
poised, wing to wing, in percussive constellations,
a gaunt orchestra gathered to guide you home.

Poverty
by Hannah Gates

Broke minded people do broke minded things
I am robbed of my innocence and relinquished with jealousy
The pain I devour breaks my heart like the inside of a piggy bank
Confused is how I feel but lost is too common
I've found my place but I cannot stay grounded
I see things that nobody else sees,
The pain that our world is going through really upsets me
But for some reason, no one seems to notice when we're empty
Deprived of our love, growth, and self-being
Sometimes being broke minded makes us do broke minded things
Like how the beginning and end of a sentence deserve to heard,
Some people refuse to use their voice because they're scared
They were not taught to be proud and to be loud,
But to cover their selves with blankets and shells
Like the outside of hell...
They welcome the innocent and seem to forget how hard they had worked
Before they gave up in the end
So my point is,
Broke minded people do broke minded things, what are we going to do
To change the way we see?

It being summer
by Christopher Alexander Gellert

i

Expect men to murder other men
with greater need,
SALT PEANUTS and
women. In winter
men take life by the hand
and drop it.

Subways bump
to cut breath.

ii

It being summer,
sex parades
where there are beaches,
where there are not,
order it :

At the bar,
with a twist.
In a box, from a fox.

Clink the ice in your glass
enough times
for the kid at the end of the bar
to polish your leer.

Rocks turn to puddles.

iii

Why are you clothed?—
save on the electric bill.

In winter, no need
for the jeer of window-shades.

iv

It being summer,
there's ice-cream.

On the Road
by Ken Gradomski

Realer than real, super-real, surreal; these are descriptive words true to early November. In vivid sunlight, I drive along the roadways top down, albeit cool, I can only think in colors... I pass by a roadside tree with its deep, brown trunk and it becomes a mast for the incandescent orange-leaf sail atop...

Red, red, red, mercurochrome, deep dark green, black shadows, all a mélange, an amalgam and I try to be that perfect Autumn picture, myself and thus become a polyglot of observant peace; each color, each scene nourishment for my soul. Then I envision my soul and it presents as a great bird flying high

above the river
above the valleys...
I soar,

I stretch my wings aloft, I yearn to love more, be more, connect more... At this moment of flight, I endure a thorough re-iteration of myself where I am merely a small paint stroke in a more than magnificent Divine canvas, a very large canvas, a dynamic canvas. And I am reassured. And I am content.

Too soon my surreal state of mind fades away until I am simply
back in my convertible riding down the road.

The Dancer
by Michael Grover

Beautiful & elegant
This cosmic dancer
Beautiful to watch her dance through the night
But she dances in cycles of abuse
Beautiful to watch from a distance
How chaotic the dance
I the weary spectator
Knowing this dance is too sad & heavy
To move forward
& she's dancing in quicksand

The Tao of Scrubbing Bubbles™
by Jennifer Hambrick

It is only a bathtub
a toothbrush
a swathe of cleanser.
It is three to five minutes
of meditation
of listening
to the crescendo of crackling
bubbles in foamy spray.

Now it is time.

I kneel
draw tiny circles
with nylon bristles
become one
with the bubbles
scrubbing, scrubbing away
the stain of world.
It is a koan
evidently beyond the ken of husbands:
Working hard so one doesn't have to
doesn't mean one doesn't have to work at all.

A stream of water from the faucet
swirls yin-yang with
depleted foam.
The residue of world
circles the drain
then disappears.

Our Lovely Lady
by Richard Harries

Nine years ago
She came into our lives
And over the years we came to truly love her
In fact we loved her straight away
She was immediately a great support to me
When I was working in a stressful job
Always there
Always reliable
Never let me down
A single time
Do not know how I would
Have managed without her

When I retired her support continued
She carried me along with her reliability
And when we made the move to the coast
It was she who was there for us
And helped us move, transported so much for us
Her dependability
And steadfastness
Were always there, always evident
And I knew that I could rely totally on her

She was brilliant even when I was not around
And Eileen trusted her as much as I did
Her colouring was lovely indeed
With a rosy blush so bright
And beautiful
And yet she started to get elderly
It became apparent
It was so evident
Developed a problem getting going in the morning
In cold weather was much less dependable
Her support for us was getting weaker
And she started costing us money
As problems occurred again and again
Then she there were even days when she could just not move

Her skin started bubbling
In an unsightly way
There seemed to be no treatment for this
And we knew that the end of the road was near

So yes
We took the plunge
And traded her in
And got a new car!
Bless our old Cherry— Petula
Now on her way to that car scrap yard ... in the sky!

Cleveland Homeless Poem
by Charles Robert Hice

in the blink of an eye Jesus shall return
the poor all gone, nowhere to turn
the benches in the park divided with an iron rung
in the middle to stop them lying down
these are the end times the world is worshipping the devil
Satan has come in the form of the phone number
666-Cleve-me
the men can't walk without aid
the drinks flow every midnight every day
the price of Jesus is about three dollars now
a coffee four
food is not even priced
if you have to ask them do not go inside
let the clothing rot, let the skin maggot
these are the days foretold by the King
these are the end
nothing works unless paid for with money
COIN of the realm, paper and silver and GOLD
angels fly near to me inserting credits up my feet
why did eye have to be so homeless, they gasp
nothing fits your feet
eye am saved and eye am invincible, nothing probes
nothing moves inside of me but love
a parody of
Bukowski
credits in my eye
money in my brain
debits in my feet
spent like a flower in the prance
first name Charles
last name OHIO

Afternoon Assassin
by Veronica Hopkins

Objectified love
Cupid's impostor is sly
He spares none of us

That's not love, honey
Face against the heating vent
Hands to muffle screams

Love's doppelganger
Bones for breaking and fractures
Crutches and ice packs

Love can conquer all
Should one be lucky enough
Swollen face, cracked lips

Obsessive nature
Property and possession
Human ownership

Reduced by violence
Deemed a masochist by peers
Once a romantic

Paramedics watch
Hyperventilation, shock
Flowers sent to assuage

Engagement, enslaved
Arsenic for Valentines
Snow falls upon blood

Beelzebub grins
Telepathic moves in Chess
Pawns topple royals

Silence is golden

An essential element
Speak not of ruin

Holes in the drywall
Doors beaten off the hinges
Shards of glass in hand

Cringe at the prospects
Another month of hobbling
True immobilization

Lie to the doctor
We are all somewhat clumsy
Chronic falls and spills

Brutalization
Bellows to deafen the ears
Knuckle vision, blurred

Woo with words of hope
So charming in the evening
Terror in the morn

So Habanera!
That's love, just like the song says
Do tombs show the truth?

Hatred hides and waits
Preys upon the buoyant soul
Annihilation

Make your peace for good
Say a prayer and wave a blade
Save what's left of self

Sun-Tzu did not know
of such harsh tribulations
The box cutter blues.

Cupid's imposter
i.e. Love's doppelganger

now swimming in Styx

Not in the headlines
'An afternoon assassin'
What you have become

The neighbor's judgment
Reduced to a nervous smile
And a conjured laugh.

For BRI
by Alina Howard

you intrigue me
the way your silence speaks volumes
the muteness to my ear tells me how much I can confide anything to you
the stillness on your face
the way gravity wants to take over
but your melanin says other ... WISE
you raise your fist high out of knowledge
                            out of pride
you're a lion, no master can tame you
you will not hide your fro because you are fro-ocious
the minds of men QUAKE as you walk
you will never allow yourself to surrender
          to the ideologies the world wants to place upon you
you have more beauty than anyone could ever wish for
but no one wishes for such a queen only mediocrity
you are Queen derived from Egypt
                    buried amongst pharaohs
gold in your bones as rich as your melanin
I will humbly go on my knees and offer myself up to you as if you are
                                                  my only hope
you are our queen and it is an honor to be placed amongst you.

My Father Played the Door like a Steinway Concert Grand
by Christine Howey

pizzicato

Coming home just before our bedtime to say goodnight, a syncopated tapping with his fingernails on my bedroom door like he did on the steering wheel when listening to jazz. Then his scratchy kiss, his breath heavy with bourbon.

liberamente

Jerking my sister's bedroom door open and closed, each time showing us a different funny face, Suzy and I rolling on the floor giggling.

lugubre

Soft knock, a pause, then another, at the front door at 3 a.m. "Sorry. Keys are somewhere, Paul drove me home."

pianissimo

Buddy Rich on the brushes, grazing the back door with the palm of his hand to a slow beat as he says, "I have to go, but next time, next time for sure."

intimo

A playful knuckle-riff on the glass pane of the patio door, getting mom's attention with a wink on a summer afternoon. We are told to play outside and not come upstairs, under any circumstances.

fortississimo

With the heel of his hand on their bedroom door, over and over again, mom locked inside after the yelling.

vivo

Sprightly, with both hands on both sides of the swinging kitchen door, playing it like an Irish drum, propped open the morning after. After being gone all night.

bellicose

Flat hand against his den door, slam-sealing himself off from us, rattling windows in the dining room.

caesura

Maybe the best, the silence. Maybe the worst.

doloroso

Three neatly separated knocks on the basement door. "Come upstairs, kids. Mom and I have to talk to you."

Summertime Memory
by Dionne D. Hunter

Grass tickles my bare feet
Warm sun beats down on caramel shoulders
Sounds of children playing, jumping, laughing carry on the breeze
Not a care in the world other than 1st one back wins
Beads of sweat drip from my brow and taste salty on my lips
Laughter grows louder LOUDER
I yell, I think I found it
—A four leaf clover— could it be?
Running back, fast
Leaping over clouds
I feel like I've already won
Adult calls out, Game over, Dionne found it
Waves of joy rush over me
I think this feeling will never end
The prize, who remembers, not me and it doesn't even matter
I just enjoy remembering how the grass tickled my toes and how the sun
    beat down on caramel skin and the laughter, so much laughter
Oh how I miss the innocence of just being a kid

Silent as a Star
by Clarissa Jakobsons

For days, it is January still, fresh snow
has fallen on this gray Ohio landscape.
The voice at the end of the line is not you.
It announces your final breath was released
last week in that wind-boxed city.

Weeks ago, we spoke ten minutes at a time.
Sometimes your cough erupted
a tired disclosure, while the ventilator
trailed a monotonous out-of-tune soliloquy.

Late—missed again. If only
I had reminded you of my birth date
perhaps you'd have taken another breath?
But, my birth and your ashes are forever
marked, united by prayer.

I did not call soon enough, dearest Guna.
Bleak January after the Christmas rush,
drawn days escape. Off-white sky
bagged in silence and farewells
want words that slipped away.

Hello, you say—lost day ends
gray as it began, here in Ohio.
I listen for the drizzle, sleet, some
snow, and that fateful call—
silent as a star.

Silent as a star refers to Daniel Thompson.

You Are My Solar System
by Azriel Johnson

My soul insistence
Your eyes are moons
Your limbs are trajectories
of planetary fingers and toes
Your head is the universal connection
with hair tendrils stretching
light years
Your openings are black holes
transforming chemicals
with organic fusion, intense
pressure and bending the space-
time continuum to process
drawing nutrients and spiritual energy
Your heart pushes the energy through
I watch you orbit, you rotate
on an axis of love and you turn
my life into something revolutionary

The Call of the Water
by Chuck Joy

my eyes seek the restfulness of water
any blue surface, stirred or placid

remember a former distant war?
stopping communism on the Korean peninsula

the confusions of Europe thoroughly subdued
everything ruined over there

the redbrick hospitals of Cleveland
echo the glee of the newborn, keep 'em warm

that winter lasted well into June
men froze in basements, their dreams extinguished

Ginsberg shivered in a threadbare parka
running errands for his friends at Columbia

radio was king, radio and trains
telephone cords plugged into switchboards

young people cared about one thing, sleds
hockey was played in four cities and Canada

those newborns, every one, unconcerned
their immediate needs drove all their behavior

only later did they recognize the needs of others
the hardknock life, the call of the water

Cat Nap
by Stan Kaufman

Our cat found a sunny spot of carpet to nap on.
As the sun gets higher, the spot moves
      And soon she's in the shade.
She rises, looks about, stretches, then takes a
      Few steps to the East and resumes her nap
         In the sun.

But soon she's in the shade again
      And the process repeats.
When the sun gets high enough the
      Spot disappears altogether!

Then she rises and glares at me
      As though it's my fault!
She bathes a bit and then,
      Having napped up enough energy,
      She stalks off – looking for trouble!

Consider the Junco
by Sue Kaufman

He has flown long miles from the Arctic north
to spend his winter in Ohio.
Most birds fly south to warmer climes
when snow drifts and temperatures descend.

But not this perky dark-eyed junco.
He loves Ohio's bleak winters.
I, coffee cup in hand,
watch as his smoky cowl and cloak and twiggy legs
move around the feeder, pecking at seeds,
as the blustery wind ruffles his feathers.

He fluffs his wings to carve seed and snow
and makes ramparts to keep the wind away.
I shiver just watching him,
and wonder, "Why, oh why vacation here, little bird?"

Midsummer Night Walking with Daniel Thompson
by Diane Kendig

At sunset we note
the local Crazy Man
circling and recircling the block,
a June 22nd so hot,
it's dog days a month early.

Our two dogs run and duck
while we, dog-tired, play watch-dogs,
smile, forget ourselves;
we've gone to the dogs,
and they'll let us lie.

"Why 'Emma' for your new dog's name?"
he asks. "It means 'healer'," I say.
"Like on a leash?"
"Like in a wound."
"Maybe she'll do both."

The sun bleeds to its place
on this longest day.
From now on, shorter, darker.
And the real heat.
I follow Emma home.

Miyazhane Vance
by Kim theBwordpoet

From their sleep they are taken in the dark.
Their portals closed from exposure,
The sounds of 10 pops;
Where is mommy?

Dressed in their Sunday best,
Things return to normal
Except somebody should be with us...
Where is mommy?

Out of the mouths of babes
Comes the yell of the confused.
Their eyes hold a question;
Where is mommy?

Senselessness turns into intrusion.
Malicious intent turns into deadly action.
Now she lays red in her bed;
Snatched from this world.

In Medias Res
by Mindi Kirchner-Greenway

Because beginnings promise to be unbearable—
think phonic tics, a hole in my mouth
where words should be,
or the flooded blood
and bone-twist of a difficult birth—
I'm dragging the middle toward you.

Doctor, chirps just-fertilized egg,
I'm finished starting—
toss me into this world mid-life and sullen
sign me up for an unpaid mortgage,
and an ex-everything

because I want anonymous,
continuously—none of this
but I'd really like to know you better banality
because I want the way your eye blinks
in pentameter,

I want sing-song and chant:
I love coffee,
I love tea,
I love the boys and they love me.

It's all heart-sputter and sweat in here, honey,
because I want history stripped naked,
pages torn until all that's left is now.

Because I want
living and living
and living,
all the while,
without ever having
to be born.

Sanguine
by Paul Koniecki

sometimes flowers are blue
sometimes stars are yellow

sometimes oceans are green
or choppy like the

salt inside of me
and i wonder if

waves had hands would
water cut itself open

to be free sometimes
the answer in the

air is just more
air and a chance

for another faraway tomorrow sometimes death is a

lie as silver as
the moon to guide

us and the mind
inside my mind does

not mind and the
world is a statue

without arms sometimes clouds break apart and bleeding

die sometimes the sky
is pink sometimes all

i want is us
in the night to

blot your tears with
my cheeks my lips

my tongue lost in
the day indivisible yellow

cupping desperation of our
pink deliverance sometimes i

want to live forever
sometimes the sky is me

Orders
by Leonard Kress

Sometime, sooner or later
you'll have to make the journey.
You might think you don't have a clue
where to begin, but you do
know, you've always known the place.
You might have read about it in Pausanias,
who traversed the whole of Greece,
mountains, plains, and seas to find it—
what he called the Oracle of Trophonius.

But that was his, not yours
and you can't just repeat his descent,
the inhaled forgetfulness and stiff-necked sentries,
lunging head-first into the cave's tight hug.
He survived, though barely,
which is all you can expect—
the bewilderment that persists
long after your return. Finding the place
to enter is the hardest. What's certain is
that you'll stumble in, caught off-guard,
perhaps be shoved. It might take
wine or sex to throw your kilter off,
or being fired or breaking up,
anything to evict you from ease and succor.

You'll feel like hot glass thrust
into the glory hole. No doubt
you'll melt, become pliable,
expand with a breath not your own.
But you will not shatter, and once
your life returns, you'll recognize others
who've gone before—a glint in their eyes,
pleas not to press for details.

Examination of a Rainbow
by Tom Kryss

Now some will say that I have debauched its integrity
by bringing it up on the screen, that we should have
left it back there in the skies and blue veins. I wish
it were true that such powers remanded. Now

I can zoom in on it, if I like, and reduce it to an arrangement
of pixels a little like Mondrian's squares, but a great deal
less than Cezanne, certainly not in the least reminiscent
of the optimism of sunflowers. No, I prefer not to reduce it
by enlargement, or enlarge it to the ridiculous extent
that I have no idea what I am staring at. One should be happy
to see it just as it was. *Just as it was?*

Why has it taken on the corporeality of the aluminum gutters
by which, side by side, it appears? Where is the sense that each
wavelength has been drawn to a specific relation with its counterparts
and locked into place? Where, indeed, are the backfiring — entirely
inferred — sweeps of the hand which attempted containment?
Where are you? Where am I?
WHERE IS THE STREET?
You almost had to view it in terms of the street and I don't know why
so much is missing.

Clouds were running in under it. Time conspired against it.
You chased it down to the middle of the street and stood there and fought
  with it
as if it were an unimaginably large kite filled with some type of helium.
But it looked like you got it, grinning at the miniature camera,
holding the viewfinder, backwards, right up to your eyes.

And There Was Stillness
by Lori Ann Kusterbeck

in the wee morning hours
before society yawns and opens its eyes
a solitary soul drives

and there was stillness

in those hours
the road stretched on
the last of his kind
a wanderer
drifter logging the miles
through the wounded land of his past
his present just a blur of city limit signs
future glimpses of visions

contentment only found on the open road
away from the city smog
far from suit coats and mad men
far from sad children and had women
undeveloped land
trees after trees after empty fields

there was stillness

his was no forceful rebellion
abandoning all he was taught to try for
all that he was hypnotized to die for
all that he was forced to lie for

no

he befriended the road
the kindness of strangers
his backseat his bed
sleeping under the open stars
in the arms of stillness.

Four Skunks
by Jill Lange

At twilight,
as the fireflies awaken,
four skunks meander
nose to tail
through my yard.

Three carry wide white stripes
from tip of head
to bushy tail.

The fourth wears his stripe upside down,
sports a skinny black tail
and ... Oh! ... a collar around his neck.

My cat, Dance!

Haiku
by Phyllis Lee

first time
hearing Mama's laughter
in mine

Vocabulary Lesson
by Lennart Lundh

Here. She pointed.
Touched my lips, her collarbone,
again my lips.

The clavicle,
from Latin: *clavicula*,
"little key."

The key to?
She touched her sternum,
said, *make no bones*.

Triptych
by Susan Mallernee

morning rain
my mother's babushka
neatly folded

hospice store
seeing my mother's
clothes again

all morning
the linens mother saved
for someday

The Future of Medicine
by Marc Mannheimer

moment by moment
we see the healing of all wounds
in all beings of all worlds
with no insurance
without a prescription

with hands
over hearts
hers and yours
braided together

the 3 ingredients
in the poultice they hold

infinity
quaking
mud

Sunset in the Rain
by Julie Ursem Marchand

The patter of falling rain on the leaves
of the lilac bush outside the open kitchen window
blends a cool groove to the reggae beats
flowing from The Dirty Heads CD that
I popped in the player to keep me company
while washing dishes.
My hips sway to these rhythms
until the drying rack is full and I
plop a pan under the suds to soak.
I shimmy towards the window to
listen to the rain pour from the gutters
and catch a breath of fresh air.

The leaves of the lilac bush gleam
the silvery reflection of the clouds above.
The belly of the clouds in the distance
are illuminated in a blushing coral
by the setting sun.
As the clouds begin to glow brighter
before the day draws to an end,
I think perhaps there may be a
rainbow on the other side of the house,
but I cannot bring myself
to leave such glory and beauty.

I lean on the refrigerator and
can almost feel the earth roll
as I watch the sky transform
itself from a golden peach
to the slate blue and violet
before it fades to black.
The music has stopped,
but my heart still
sways to the
rain tumbling
from the sky.

Moving Skylines
by Elizabeth Marino

Heading for Chicago out on Highway 41,
a grainy radio station starts a-wailing out
You've Got to Lively Up Yourself and
a pretend badness — *I'm Special* — across
crew-cut wheat fields of a depressed land
all the air and snakes beneath its surface
smoothed out years ago.

Up and across from tropical
Bloomington, Indiana
with its hot and heavy air
that's good for softening skin
and drawing plants up thick-
stemmed and wide-leaved
from undulating hills.
> *My notebook tracked*
> *a midsummer full moon shining down*
> *down there on us not sleeping*
> *through the shortest night of the year.*

The horizon keeps coming and falling back —
the shapes of places that serve grits
and cream gravy on white Styrofoam,
hills brushed with pale lavender flowers
Scottish heather,
a peacock challenging traffic
from a fork in the road.
> *You kept commenting on my famous Chinese*
> *('Two billion feet can't be wrong') slippers:*
> *"Those must be pretty stylish down in Chicago.*
> *I just started seeing 'em up in Milwaukee."*

The nights are longer now. August heat
rising, wrinkles the street lit air.
I crack open my airshaft window.
The blues drift in, cool
from the bass player downstairs

urging me to linger —
> *Sweet Home, Chicago*
> *Sweet Home, Chicago.*

Love is a Carcass
by Jonie McIntire

A roasted grocery chicken,
purchased as dinner
with a coupon about to expire,
fills the car in steam.
The smell seeps in before
the front door is fully open
and the children run up,
eagerly hungry.

We barely make it to the table —
our savage fingers
dripping flesh into our mouths.
Our lips glisten smiles
and you walk in, laughing —
look at us!

We talk, cheeks full,
of the time with the fish
on the grill, whole
with his eyes and us
circling with forks.

Then another time with
snow forts, the second baby
coming home, and earlier,
to the first baby —

and all the while
both kids chime in with
memories they don't have
but heard. They are
wide-eyed and we have talked
back, long before the work
left and the bills
turned red,
before we two became
we four, back

to our audacious wedding,
only fifteen minutes long
with flies and hayrides,
and the Sharon Olds poem
and how we refused to explain
that moo shu pork
is a vow, that love is a carcass.

Our fingers are filthy
and we find rags
to wipe them off,
the four of us
rubbing our bellies,
placing bones in water
to make tomorrow's soup
from the juice.

Cut to the Quick
by Sarah McIntosh

There is no cutting to be done—
I am the quick, the tingling nerve,
the tongue-tang of fine wine.
Dopamine floods my veins
like spirits palming walls,
espresso perpetual.

I am a resetting thermostat,
relearning heat beneath my skin—
slack and soft, sheer curtains rippling
open the morning.

I am a nervous machine,
chainsaw legs sawing oaks
and wood-chipper eyes grinding up
tenacity and tact.

My epicenter rocks me to sleep;
on occasion, shock waves jolt me
into earthquake shudders, seismographic
etchings, frequencies frantic.

I am the quick:
split middle, melted-ice puddle,
condemned embers, shifted logs rekindled.
Spark and stutter, string plucked,
bark-peeled sycamore
exposed to the teeming, green spring.

I am dandelion blow ball,
twitchy wind that carries it.
I condense into droplets of water
and cling to anemone flowers,
and I am the bud never broken.

Leave me be
and I'll bloom
into my own presence.

Segue Way Burque
by Frankie Metro

Segue way meter maids on
Gold Avenue appear w/ badges,
Blue lycron polymer helmets & crotch level, motorized
Battering rams. It's a brisk pace up 4 blocks
And every long bearded, fine arts major on a bicycle
Who wanders too far from the pyramidal vortex—
Where we sacrifice engaged activity while Nike enthusiasts
Provide photo ops in front of the post office/court house,
Where hatchet men w/ face tattoos find a month's worth of gravel in their
 Marlboro duffle bag,
No one's wearing derby hats & worshipping pugilism in this city, at least
 not at the frequency I'm accustomed to, instead interchanging lot space
 between hot dog carts & votive candles for the dead.
We don't hear much about horse thieves & Mayan gods buried in stalagmite
 deposits, we just rub salt over the dusty wounds & claim it's clay earth,
 paisos in xxl polos, urine soaked McDonald's loiterers/lobbyists. The
 closest thing we have to friends are sleeping in their cars or crashing at
 your pad talking the systematic downfall of traffic culture.
But everyone's mi primo, mi sangre. Everyone's first in line to watch the
 other bleed out
And be right...

At Gem City Marina
by Marisa Moks-Unger

From pier side at Gem City Marina
a family reunion of vessels takes place.
One, the Lucasaurus, is a sleek yacht triple
the size of those in the slips. She has owners
who sip Sea Breezes or Rum and Coke.

Nearby, whole fraternities of sailboats rock in
deep primary yellows, reds and blues.
They sit tight together and blow windy tales
into their sails and bob in the rough chop.
Their sailors are college-educated, who wash down Labatts.

The blue-collar boys, the working class, crowd
closely to the pier for their next assignments.
The tugs and barges move freight, sand to fill Presque Isle.
Their drivers belly up for Rolling Rocks
at Three Bs Bar-b-que or Chestnut St. Tavern.

And quite by himself, the Bay Patrol boat,
set apart like an odd, old uncle who falls asleep
during dinner conversation. Provider of protection.
Not sleek, nor snobby. Not sloppy — existing only to serve.
His owner downs Maxwell House morning, noon and night.

"Outta Breath" Seth
by Anne Marie Moore

The following is an educational story for pediatric asthma patients, geared for preschool-through primary school-aged children. It gives information about many of the symptoms, causes, and treatment for asthma using simple language that young children can understand.

Now, Seth was a typical 6-year-old kid;
He enjoyed all the games that the other kids did.

At recess, he'd be on the playground each day —
But there was a problem that got in his way!

The harder he played, the more likely Seth
Wound up on the sidelines and gasping for breath.

His lips would turn blue, and his heart would beat fast;
The game would break up 'til the episode passed!

Seth felt like his insides would get really tight —
And not only that — it got worse in the night!

A terrible cough kept him up all night long;
His family all knew that something was wrong!

It got even worse when his aunt was around —
Her smoking caused Seth to cough *more*, it was found.

His mom finally figured — enough was enough!
A doctor would get to the root of this stuff!

She made an appointment the very next day
To see what the pediatrician would say.

Well, Seth didn't know if he liked this or not;
Would the doctor be mean? Would he give him a shot?

But he needed to breathe, so he gave his consent;
He summoned his courage. To the doctor's he went!

The nurse and the doctor turned out to be *nice*!

They talked and they listened. Some things, they did twice.

The nurse asked a whole lot of questions of Seth —
Like, what he was *doing* when he ran out of breath?

She wanted to know . . . Did his fam'ly have pets?
Did they live on a farm? Did they smoke cigarettes?

She listened for sounds that his chest made, and then
The doctor came in — and he listened again!

The doctor examined and tapped on his chest
And ordered an x-ray and lung function test.

Then finally, the doctor announced he was sure
Seth suffered from *asthma* — (which he couldn't cure);

But he could supply him with things that he'd need
To make his life go a lot smoother, indeed!

The doctor sat down and explained lots of facts
About certain things that caused asthma attacks.

His aunt's cigarettes were a trigger, he knew —
But Seth was surprised to learn other things, too —

Would trigger his asthma — like pet hair and mold,
And changes in weather (most often the cold)!

He guessed that some problems with germs would exist —
But even just *getting upset* made the list!

When Seth left the doctor's, he felt pretty wise;
He knew a lot more, and was armed with supplies —

Like medicine that he would take every day
To help keep his problems with breathing at bay.

He had an inhaler for emergencies, too;
If there was a crisis, he'd know what to do!

He couldn't completely *prevent* an attack —
But if one occurred — well, at least he'd fight back!

Now Seth still goes out to the playground each day
But asthma can no longer get in his way.

So remember — if *you* always seem out of breath —
You might be the next "asthma expert" . . . like Seth!

Recipe for a Heartbreak
by Laura Moore

How to make a Heartbreak:

Ingredients:
3 cups of ignorance
1 tbsp. Misunderstanding
1/2 cup of carelessness
4 cups of gossip
5 tsps. Violence
2 cups problems beyond your control
A pinch of hostility
1 goodbye

Mix ingredients together, adding a dash of hatred here and there when needed. Bake in oven until completely burned. Sprinkle with broken promises. Put on a dish and serve to unsuspecting victim.

Makes 1 Broken Heart.

Note: Best when served with a cold shoulder or a hot temper. Never serve with a warm heart.

Killing You Roughly
by Tracie Morell

You are living off far more
than a single human being

could possibly need
to live pleased,

peacefully. Some say that it's a life

of excess. I call it excessive indifference
to every Other around. You don't care

to think about how sometimes
their hands are so rooted in their eyes

from the cruel order of indifference
to human suffering, because you are too busy

reflecting on your own desires. Entire nations could
die denied their own name for the sake of your personal

gain. You let yourself be
ruled by the inhumanity of consumer

economics instead of the careful nurture
home economics could offer you. How

many fine suits and luxuriously made silk
scarves do you have? You know the ones so nice

to the touch making the hand slide down your chest
like Narcissus caressing yourself. Psychoanalysts say

it's typical psychopathy of the tendrils, pedals, orange on
white dying in a reflecting pond having been cut

from their very root system. Psychotherapy may be useful
to mollify the narcissistic personality to relate to others

less manipulatively, but there is no cure. It's known that
they can't cure you of that vanity staring right back to you

from your vanity standing in your gaze—the exquisite
craftsmanship of that fine wood encasing the looking

glass. You are your own portrait so you need not
commission one. Too deluded with willful ignorance

to one's own self-serving behavior—always ready, willing to
convict and sentence anyone who doubts his

greatness. Watch as I light that fine furniture on fire
just to watch your image go up in flames.

Whale Bus Schedule
by Leah Mueller

In 1900, an artist saw a twenty-first century
where people strap trolleys
to the bellies of whales, and ride beneath them
on underwater excursions. The whale
is a mere conveyance, and swims impassively
through the subterranean currents
like a horse with a hundred saddles.

The commuters are unimpressed
by the improbability of their transport
as they wait for their stops with impatience,
angry that once again, the whale is running late.
Exhausted, they stare through the windows
at passing seaweed, neon fish, and anemones
that can't stop waving at the whale bus
no matter how many times they see it.

The passengers clutch their briefcases and grocery bags
and watch carefully as each stop arrives.
They swim away, oxygen tanks securely attached,
while new people enter the whale bus,
fold up their tanks like umbrellas, then
place them beside their feet in neatly folded piles,
careful not to make too much of a mess.

No one knows what the whale is thinking.
God-like, he floats near the surface,
trolley dangling underneath: his body
is the cable that holds the world together.
The passengers trust that he won't let go
and send them plummeting to the ocean floor,
and he doesn't disappoint-he even arrives early
to his final destination, and has a few extra minutes
for a smoke before he has to turn around
and start the journey all over again.

The Rollins Band Concert
by Elliot Nicely

On the collapsing edge of uncertainty
watching innocence descend into an abyss of
steaming violent rapture where
electrolytes drown any hope for air
I was struggling, gasping, grasping, wanting
to embrace more of the warrior-poet's call to
arms that dripped from the tips of canine teeth
piercing my body and my mind like
ink needles that were overflowing and
running down my leg.

Breathe. Swallow. It's over.

Sane
by Tanya Pilumeli

i.

Sound mind.
The sound must be a hush not
a rushing. It must be a hum not
a roar. Drumroll of centipede feet
like lock-steps up your spine. Not
arrhythmia like the patter of leaves falling
in a storm.
Never a storm, more a pot-hazed parade
of soft air pulling up
then down. A stirring of a sugar spoon just so
to make the coffee sweet. Don't
clink, just that tug of motion as you stir.

ii.

Can you taste that elephant sweat that you cannot see? Oh, God, it's dripping across your face, so much brine I can smell it from here. Please don't touch me, don't hold me. Please don't. Your eyes are so dark how do they see? Icy olives sweating like horses. Just dripping your brains everywhere. How do you see? Why aren't you drained? Fallen? A walking dead in a black t-shirt? Kiss me.

iii.

Hinged. Settled. Holophrenic. Not
to be split, moving, swinging. Not
to be unsound, silent. not
psychosis, not animation of the soul, not
to rip open and spill onto the floor for everyone to see.
A door with a lock, a house with a foundation. Not
a moth by a light, not a hummingbird wing, not
psychopathic, not too much empathy, sympathy, not
the soul swinging, not
split not
deranged, fallen out of order, puzzle with a lost piece, not

shifty, shifting. Rock, but do not fall
off your rocker.

iv.

I can't hear you. I don't want to. Your lips are moving but I can't. I can see
you with my eyes closed. If I look at you that way your skin starts to melt. I
found a yellowed letter from myself and keep it in my pocket. It said I would
meet you and I would hate you. I don't read it. If I open it again, the folds
will split. I remember, though, what you wrote. The ink is almost gone. You
wrote me the letter so long ago. Do you remember?

v.

Zipped. Each metal tooth locked. No
key to insert. A neat handle to not pull. Nothing
like Don Quixote. A tap, not
a rattling. A tap. A tap. A tap. A tap.
like a drop falling repetitively. In the center
without touching the sides. Falling though the center, but not
falling. Staying in your mind, but not
touching the sides. Listen to the tap, tap, tap get louder
as you stir. The echo will drive you back in.

vi.

Again. Please, again. Show me that again. Don't forget I hate you.

Spiritual Mind Design
by Alois Polzer

I can fathom down to the atoms
then rearrange into a mentally deranged uncaged sage
on a lyrical rampage incinerating my rage
now transforming it into the words on this page.
Mage magic becomes a habit when you are no longer
following but leading that elusive white rabbit
to the realm souls inhabit—the habitat of pure energy,
existing with the clarity and certainty synergizing
with the Universe in Its Totality.
Manifesting This is the revolutionary paradigm typicality.
Premonition intermission: envision the precision of the cognition technician
with metaphysical senses heightened—Enlightened.
The haze clears and the maze falls.
Superlative benevolence is protocol.
Quid pro quo synchronizing with your shadow
going with the flow and the tempo in the temple
that is our body. Then switch gears getting rogue rowdy:
Materializing mischievous manifestations of the manic mind.
All the while never blind in the third eye
with Chakras connected from the Earth to the starry
Celestial infinite sky
becoming Who, What, When, Where, and Why.
So now I ask, "What now?"
Take a vow to radiate Truth somehow.
Then just levitate and take a meditative bow
in the Universal Energy Powwow.

Ripple, Ripple
by Tam e. Polzer

She'd sneak, slip in naked,
make not one ring, one wave,
thinking she must behave that way
to protect the pond's perfection.
She didn't know then
that the pond
craved waves,
a stirring up,
a mixing of the water—
a notion that
motion made things grow
never flowed through her mind
until—
a fish jumped and splashed,
shattered its reflection—
ripple.
A hawk spotted,
swooped down,
caught and killed the fish for food—
ripple, ripple.
Frog's eggs
laid on a leaf
slipped off to a spot
between two rocks
where tadpoles were safe
to grow—
ripple.
She stood so
exposed in the sun,
vulnerable,
alone,
until she dove
from the platform,
escaping her silent turmoil on top,
to the bottom of the pond where
she enjoyed its cool depth—
her depth.

Then she pushed off a rock
and swam to the pond's middle
where she,
spreading her legs and arms wide,
cheek deep,
balanced a backfloat,
allowing her loins
and lips
and fingertips
enjoy the massage
of her own rings,
her own waves—
ripple, ripple.

The Garden Ball
by Valentina Ranaldi-Adams

The crabapples decorated the dance floor with white petals.

The woodpecker tapped a rhythmic beat.

The wind chimes played a tinkling melody.

The periwinkle wore green accented with blue florals.

The skunk was a fashion icon in a black tux and a white tie.

The azalea showed off a corsage of vibrant pink.

The rabbits danced a frantic hip-hop.

The arborvitaes did a hula in leaf-patterned shirts.

The squirrels took part in a lively jive.

The gnome chaperoned it all with a glassy stare.

Tweets Song
by Brianna Robinson

It starts with a note, bass maybe treble
Then comes the sound, an idea, a new level
It may be bright or shallow or warm sounding
Emphasizing your true feelings
Refusing to be ignored
A genuine emotion with a strong foundation
Music to my ears
It may be confused with noise,
Carrying the most distinct melody
Vibrations heard from peaks and valleys
Once sang of God's Amazing Grace
There are divine interventions
But the harmonic nature of you will never be disrupted
Often is it said that there is strength in numbers
And of course there is strength in one.
One is the beat you came in on
Although I know little about music and its theory
I know that in music there is always a resolution
And that in a battle, there is always a winner and loser
And you won.
Death is not a loss,
But the resolution to the melodic phrase of our lives
Day by day,
Night by night
We fear the resolution
Or even search for it
But when it comes
And the pitches all match
The phrase could not be more harmonic
Tones finally match up
The contest between the rhythms and blues
Has been won.

Hint of Clarity and Freedom
by Melissa Rose

I notice the debris first
an irregular wandering line of plastics
oddly too often
it consists of dullish pink tampon applicators
then the smell
I'm looking for that hint of clarity and freedom
and I get sewage flavored with fish and dead stuff
and I'm deathly allergic to fish
each step sinks deeper
trudging
holding me with the edge
I want to stop walking parallel alongside the shadow of the sun
stop the path of the land and see the bigger picture
I want to swallow the horizon and feel the whole of where I am
I want to find a spot to dig my bare toes into small sudsy stones polished
    smooth and bite size by time
find the jagged blue green water against the infinite sky
winds whip up pressing through the stench
the scent of change
inhale-able
I don't know if the tide is coming in or out
today the waves lack aggression
only the steady heavy rhythm pushing back n forth
there is a swell in my chest as I rest on an awkward piece of driftwood
my dam failing
my choked down pain and disillusionment
the peaks and valleys of feeling
crushed garbage compacted
I want the water to consume
overwhelm
to roar in heavy primal crashes
to swallow up the shore of its
injured demands and unfulfilled desires
but it hits in typical uneven heartbeats
the suck pull bulge
crest smash down repeating breath
carrying away only some of it

but some of it
wave after wave
sigh after sigh
and all I really did was turn and face the sea

Phonie
by Damian Rucci

Sometimes I feel like a big phonie.
Sometimes I think this is just another thing

I'll scratch off my "been there, tried that list"
like the radio show and the band and the career

that never seemed to come together, but words
words have always carried me through dark times

when the drugs are gone and the drink
is gone and I'm left with myself for once

I turn to these words and shape them
into something and sometimes they're good

sometimes they flow from morning to night
and I wear grooves in the black chicklet keys

but nights like tonight I'm hunched over
beating my face into the stubborn keyboard

screaming into the mirror atop my desk
"where are the words, why won't they come?"

and there's never an answer back to the screams
only more blank screen and a blinking cursor

so I turn to my drug-dealer, the one who keeps
letting me know he has "good shit and good deals"

I empty the capsules on the desk, run through the lines
and I'm back! Resurrected as pure creative energy!

And then when that is gone, like it always is
I am left with myself, unable to write again.

"Spring Fashion Modeled by Rising Young Poets"
— *O* (The Oprah Magazine)

by Rikki Santer

Stock the shelves with shrink
wrapped metaphors. The Poetnistas
are here. Each pronounced a connoisseur,
cherry-picked from the stacks. Each packaged,
full-paged and ankle deep
in her very own reflecting pool.
What eight goddesses who write poems
are wearing.

She Verbs now She Nouns.
Their verses pervert into accessory, sink
into sand, stretch across a megaphoned
hard-on, are knifed and forked
on a porcelain plate. *Her zen minimal is
channeled through the clean lines of
a French-cuffed shirt. The teal,
peach and chartreuse of a pencil
skirt and sequined cardigan make
her feel va-va-va voom.*

Frame us, too, salacious
window lickers fit for a fitting
room where beatnik turtlenecks
and black toreador pants hang
whimpering on another clever hook
of commodity.

Do It Now!

by Sharon M. Senal

It is easy to put off till tomorrow,
But we should "do it now"!
Whenever we feel lazy,
We should remind ourselves somehow.

If we put off till tomorrow,
What we can do today,
Our work will *never* get done,
It will mount higher each day.

Then we will get frustrated,
And not know where to start,
Our jobs will become endless,
Because laziness played its part.

So every time you catch yourself,
Putting things off for a day,
Stop yourself and say instead,
NO, I'll "do it now" - *TODAY!*

Untitled
by Elizabeth Senn

I've got scars that can't be spied,
I've got trauma that can't be stolen.
Longtime friend of tortured passion,
My ambition: my assassin.

I've got dreams that won't be known,
I've got memories of time unspent.
Longtime foe of a familiar hand,
My comfort: my contempt.

Ocean Potions
by Aisha Marie Smith

Ocean potion, the ocean is full of potions
Ocean potion, the ocean is full of potions that carry my emotions
As the ocean releases my emotions it causes commotion
The waves are coming in and out
Should I keep it all in or let it all out
Chime, chime, all I have is time
Time, time, I cannot get you out my mind
Mind is time, it's less than a dime
I have so much time
Tick tock, Tick tock
There goes the clock
Decisions, decisions
I only have one decision
As I close my eyes I have a vision
With my heart open I'm on a mission
Ocean potion, ocean potion
My heart is full of emotions
What do I say
Should I stay
Or should I go
Ocean potion, the ocean is full of potions
My heart is full of emotions
Should I stay with my heart in place
Or go far away with dismay?
What is there left to say?
As soon as I go my heart will be gray
Sway, sway, the sway of the waves
There goes my heart drifting away
Ocean potion, the ocean is full of potions
My heart is full of emotions
Look at all the commotion
Even though I try to give great devotion
It causes an explosion
Explosion, explosion
Suddenly you left me broken
Broken, my heart is now broken
Ocean potion, ocean potion
The ocean is full of potions
Carrying away all of my emotions

Numbers Count
by Kevin Frederick Smith

Democracy is an equation:

The Left and the Right must be made equal in order to solve problems.

We share a Common Core
yet the digits of outliers past their prime
work to multiply our divisions.

A solution can be derived by subtracting
from the exponential power
of the lesser percent.

The odds may not be even
but rational fractions.

Adam's Villanelle
by Rob Smith

Now here is this little brother of mine,
who, in early days was easily caught
when running such games as brothers will find.

Imagination drew away his mind
during hours when he was lost in thought
still, he was this little brother of mine.

And yet, there were always games in our time
of baseball and kickball and matches fought
while running such games as brothers will find.

At night, when awake, each would share our mind
across our bedroom in deep darkness wrought
still, he was this little brother of mine.

With the light came school, lessons, and work in kind,
but always, home again with comfort sought
when running such games as brothers will find.

So now, he lies close to death and we bind
the many long years lived so far apart
still, he is this little brother of mine,
and we run such games as brothers will find.

Creation Mist
by Steven B. Smith

Whole bunch of what-if maybe theories
on the how what why where when
of us, this, that, everything, nothing,
imaginary numbers, what's normal,
what's warm, what's real, what's what.

Such as we're all holograms
pre-programmed and pre-tuned
and proof lies in the low rumble static
left over from the enchantment.

Or we crawled from mud to sea to land
to be one in evolution
to which I say
"Are we not men?"

Then there's the six day magic act
creating questionable design
which in the beginning was word
but now's just plain weird
and really not working all that well.

Of course there's the no-causers
with their no beginning
and no end in explanation.

Some say we fell from the sun
as we reached for the moon
slowly eaten month by month
then regurgitated into three kingdoms
each with its own bell
which oozes into sometimes heaven
sometimes hell.

Raven talks one tale,
coyote cons another,
trickster and night ever close
with one swallowing the other.

Add in the earth divers,
chaos creation,
emergence,
the black hole spark stars,
random adaption,
the purposeful fade,
the ever expanding or soon to collapse,
men as birds and women as water,
plus the endless mirror worlds,
parallel dimensions,
alternate escalations,
the mobius becomes Sisyphus bound,
and zounds we go round again.

Yet what the why don't matter fly
cuz we still gotta try
to pay the rent
change the diaper
see what's spent
avoid the crapper
take next step
and next and next and nexter
until final chapter.

Blood still drips
tears still fall
babies always stumble
adults often appall.

So background screed matters
not at all.

Our Fall Back Position
by John Stickney

Our fall-back position is always Comrades, revolution, betrayal, compost

Our fall-back position is always redemption, Soul, parenthood, empty bottles

Our fall-back position is always almost always, words, sentences, phrases, poems, but never ever rhyme

Our fall-back position is always to alter the sleeves' length, the pant cuff, the skirt's hem, the bank balance

Our fall-back position is always to retreat from the graveyard, reach the corner of Main Street and Guilt with some dignity intact

Our fall-back position is always song and lyric, post lyric and posts about songs

Our fall-back position is always the 'Going Out Of Business Sale', the periodically empty shelves, our infra-structure's past tense, our Empire's periphery

Our fall-back position is always noise bands and apartment blocks of sound and black sea carapace

Our fall-back position is always memory's apparatus or is it the apparatus of memory or memory's apparel what you wore on that first date, the one that I do not remember

Our fall-back position is always a special committee, a select special committee, an impulse to cognitively map Committee and an impulse to cognitively conclude Committee

Our fall-back position is always to borrow another word, to slaughter the winter duck, to secure a room at the Synoptic Hotel

Our fall-back position is always, almost always cranking the windlass, forging a newly discovered Gospel, and remembering to walk don't run down the steps of Odessa

Our fall-back position is always barbaric, barbaric with a beard, barbaric with a cutlass and do-rag

Our fall-back position is always spoken of in Kongish and Singlish and Chinglish, spoken of as if percolating from below or dictated from beyond

Our fall-back position is always sublet, hostel, commune, ghost closet, defunct deep fryer left on the street

Our fall-back position is always Brian then Mick then Keith, Charlie but never Bill, only then Ron

Our fall-back position is always almost always revolution, non-revolution, uber-revolution, mis-revolution, a revolution in flavor

Our fall-back position is Father Time until at least Baby New Year stops teething

Our fall-back position is always grabbing all the chicken, geese and ducks amid the howling and lamentations caused along the way

I believe our fall-back position is our best chance for survival, this our ochre and complicated survival

Paradise
by Katherine Sturniolo

Buzzing warble
in a windowless room
the black furry
noise-maker
redirects to
synthetic radiance
tap tap
throws himself at
the translucent
barricade ceaselessly
tapping against the glass
seeking entrance
as though life
depends on it

how ignorant
you are,
fly, giving all that you have
to what will never
give back

Robert Johnson (Retold)
by Brian W. Taylor

You've heard of consenting adults
when it comes to the bedroom
but what happened to Robert Johnson —
another genius died too soon

You ask if my tale is true
Mr. Johnson I mean no disrespect
rumors can be true or false
but never what you expect

He sold his soul to the she-devil
to become king of the blues guitar
at the crossroads of good and evil
consummated the deal out back of the bar

No doubt he took the right turn
ain't no proof of heaven and hell
to become the blues guitar hero
just a sexy figment — that she-devil

In her red cat suit & tail
he spied a sultry black fox
legs long, way up to her neck
like two ribbons round a birthday box

Who knew a she-devil
Could open heaven's gate
seal the deal on a bed of flames
who'd ask for a better fate

Hey, that's your music business
you want to sell your soul to the devil
but don't hand over your body
she might just do somethin' evil

You are caught in the devil's bargain
with this lady devil in heels

you signed the line in your blood
better treat her like a lady

No double crossing
such evil in disguise
a different woman every nite
assuredly no longer wise

Rumor was jealous husband
with strychnine in wine bottle
but it was the lady devil winking
from the center of the label

No one can see crossroad signs
when you're caught in a devil's bargain
don't forget slippery when wet
dangerous curves down to hell

Sure — look over your shoulder
east and west, north and south
but when a she-devil's in your bottle
you'll pour her into your mouth

Landed
by Jonathan Thorn

Dark clouds rest in wait
In a corner of my mind
Shades of black creased by light striking
As neurons fire
Across plumes of gray matter
Rain falls softening tar
A tyrannical thick abyss
Pulling pitch at my feet
Down deep
An oppression of depression presses
My heart
My hands rise
Praising life
Waiting as silence stills

I sing in that silence
Where the night cannot hear
Dreaming of dancing through the air
With the wind at my feet

The storm brought change
Turned leaves
On the ground
Stripped the giant
Now leaving its naked fingers
To rise freely to the heavens
As its toes dig deep in the dirt
As it stands still reaching for the sky

The lofty winds that once
Carried my dreams away
Set in promises of unkempt soil
Now are firmly fitted at my feet
In a foundation where I can now grow
And rise

Hands

by Anna Marie Tokarsky

I've had time to arrange and rearrange every conversation we've ever had in my head; fast forwarding, repeating, pausing, slow motion. But there will never be a way to rewind to any of those moments, and I'm becoming okay with that. Your eyes sank into me like half smoked cigarettes in the ashtray next to our bed, and I still can't sleep when those toxins fill the air. I still can't sleep when every time I close my eyes, you're there, and I don't know whether to run to you, or run from you. Because your hands, your hands were so many things. They were the space between my shoulder blades, the part that held my posture, standing straight and strong. You told me that Your hands were meant to carve my soul into the beautiful moon and we screamed each night for a love that we may never be able to touch, but to me, that symphony turned to a lullaby. But the lullaby slowly curdled into the howling of wolves. And your hands became bullets, machine gun bullets. Colliding with my throat as your fingers constricted, your hands were the pressure and my throat was the tube of toothpaste as you're trying to get out the last drop. And instead of carving me into something beautiful, you simply carved into me. Your apologies came every morning, but your liquid happiness came every afternoon until evening, and Budweiser never made you as happy as you thought. and my dried blood on the pillows never had enough time between that small space to get run through the wash enough times to not stain. The blood was more than on those sheets. And when the house started to take on that gloom, it was as if something had died within those walls, scratching until their fingernails were filed down to the skin, trying to get out. I remember you cornering me in the kitchen, eyes sunken and turned black, hollowed out like the grave you had dug to bury our love inside, but I've paid it so many visits with roses, carnations, Passion flowers… But none of them seemed to be enough to keep your hands off me. The kitchen sink held me for a moment, washing away the part of my ribs that held me together. The floor held me for a moment, until the power in your hands traveled like a speedboat through neurons concluding with 9 swift kicks to my torso. But, of course, your hands carried me to bed when I couldn't walk for a few days. Your hands traced maps of love and poetry over the scars of the fight and the apologies came more often and more sincerely. And you always promised me that I was your moon, and I just could never quite love you like that.

When I was young, love was blankets and warmth, midnight drives with lullabies from my mother's lips, peeking through the crib rails to make sure she was still sitting in the corner of the room drifting to sleep.

Love was hanging stockings together atop the crackling embers of the fireplace, ripping through gift wrapping paper to find the dollhouse of my dreams.

Love was Indian princess meetings, because Mama and I spent too much time together, and I needed to know who my father was when she wasn't around.

Love was the birth of a baby brother, being chased down by the principal heading out to the playground for recess, to tell me that I was now a big sister and grandma was on her way to take me to the hospital. Holding him in my small arms with the help of mommy and daddy, staring into his little eyes, and promising to change every diaper, even though I didn't have it quite mastered yet, but I still wanted to try.

But love started to change when daddy wouldn't let me sleep in their bed anymore, but baby brother was allowed. Silently tugging my pillow and blankets behind me to make a nest in front of their bedroom door while the thunder and lightning rolled on through the night. I learned that I couldn't rely on anyone but myself to keep warm.

Love became hands. Love became lashes through tongue and mouth, hurting even more than the whip behind the head. Love became blame to that little boy that I once called brother, the one I promised to take care of, now took up mommy and daddy's time and I had no place. Love was pretending that it was okay on Sunday mornings and at Indian princess meetings.

Love was telling mommy that she should get rid of the baby that was in her stomach. Love was therapy on the weekends because I couldn't be around that little girl if I told mommy to get rid of her.

But then, love was looking into her bright, blue eyes, and telling her I was Anna, and even though I wasn't excited about her, I got to name her, so I loved her now. Love was really meaning that. Love was really changing her diapers, because I knew how to now.

Love was putting powder all over my face and scaring little brother.

Love was a leg, being fully extended as a friend stood nearby, and crashing down 12 steps onto a cement surface, forgetting what it was to breathe when my head hit first, slightly being able to hear him say, you deserved it, and my friend rushing out the garage door to run down the street to call her mother.

Love was not letting her call the abuse hotline. I could handle it myself, because I was a big girl and couldn't leave my siblings alone.

Love was a girl showing up on my doorstep asking to play kickball. Love was forgetting that life wasn't bad when she was there.

Love was writing.

Love was writing her poems, and her writing me poems, and we felt like everything would be okay because we had each other.

And love lasts.

Fast forward:

Love was black and white. Playing with green leaves, setting them on fire, and inhaling them through the hole of a small pipe. Love was seeing that small, dark mark on his neck that I knew I hadn't left, and pretending it wasn't there. Love was chasing him down the street the day before Valentine's Day, disregarding that I was barefoot and there was snow on the ground.

Love was skipping school, and my parents getting a restraining order against my boyfriend because they didn't like his skin color. Love was turning the corner when I saw him in the halls, and him chasing me down, fabricating a story for the mark on his neck, and leaving me for her.

Love was the rebound that went out of control, Invader Zim on the couch, and 3 years of not wanting to kiss the boy I was dating on the lips because it felt wrong.

Love was getting love back, and rejecting it, because the other boy loved me so much and slept outside my window when I wouldn't let him in.

Love was forgetting that I was a real person too, until I knew I was on my way to an emergency room for forgetting my name and running at full speed into a garage door.

Love was finding the strength to leave him, because no one was allowed to disrespect my father, even if I hated him, besides me.

Love was letters from mother in another state, recovering from an illness I couldn't explain.

Love was cooking meals so mom would eat something other than just apples and peanut butter.

Love was making mother happy because she was the only one that ever made me happy.

Love was waking up to her crawling across the bedroom floor, helping her into bed, and telling her everything would be okay.

Love was married with children, but we rolled around in sheets until his ring slipped on his finger and he told me he couldn't do this anymore.

Love was training to shoot a deadly weapon for Barrack Obama, only to have the barrel put to my head while the hand that gripped the trigger forced himself inside me like the bullet in its casing, and I screamed as I heard the gunshot collide with my body. STOP. Please. Don't.

Love was being cheated on with my best friend on Valentine's Day. Love was not finding out about it until 8 months later, along with twelve other girls. Love was hot sauce on spaghetti and sugar in Alfredo. Love was blowjobs in tattoo shops and giving someone such a purpose in life to achieve his dreams. And he did. And I'm proud.

Love was getting mom out. Love was bottles of wine and a new home at Grandma's house. Love was leaving dad, all of us.

But love was also making amends. Love was dad, finally telling me he loved me.

Love was mom, starting to get color back in her face, and seeing her smile again. Something I had so much missed since she used to sing those lullabies.

Love was my picture falling down at my boyfriend's place when there was no wind, as I took a blade to my skin, seeing his name light up on my phone because he knew something was wrong. Love was intuition about each other.

Love was graveyards in a rainstorm, and make up running down my face. Love was divorce, and helping a friend mend through his pain.

Love was hotel rooms and jersey shore. Love was yellow flowers and walks around a hotel complex. Love was sex, and sex, and sex. Love was waking up in the morning, knowing that you're expected to leave and he'll be on the couch.

But then, love turned wicked.

Love was your lovers baby being born on Valentine's Day. The one you weren't supposed to know about or acknowledge. Love was telling the baby's mother that you were sorry for not telling her you knew sooner, and still trying to put up a fight for his love.

And then, love was too fast.

Love was adult slip and slides and hiking in old man's cave. Love was 6am conversations and puppies cuddling against a man they had just met. Love was maple bacon chips, pepperoni, and provolone cheese. Love was the Beatles.

Love was not wanting to go to work because of distance, and shower conversations of how we were once two strings, but have formed into a knot, we could never be severed. Love was peeing on each other in that shower, because every serious conversation needs some humor. Love was having drunken sex while driving down the freeway at midnight.

Love was fireworks and running horses.

Love was the perfect way your hand curved around my face, the way your eyes lit up every time I entered a room

But love became arguments, arguments about work, being pushed into walls for trying to walk away in a disagreement.

Love was sinking into each other like thumbprints in hot wax during football games every night, putting all of our savings up our noses to keep us smiling radiantly.

Love was bacon roses, petals scattered across the bed

Love was trying to make up for your dicks and hands mistakes from the morning her name wasn't erased from your phone, blue light and my voice screaming get out to wake you

Love was the leg of the platform bed, singing me to sleep on Valentine's Day morning

Love was post it notes arranged in a heart on the bathroom mirror, where it said you're my hero, should've said I'm terrified of you

Love was keys thrown across the parking lot and groups of college boys telling him to "leave that little girl alone"

Love was muffling my screaming with constricted hands against my throat because the neighbors will hear.

Love was our puppy, wanting the screaming to stop, and taking it upon himself to take the lashes by pissing on our legs.

Love was jumping on top of the car as I'm trying to leave the parking lot, kicking in the windshield. Love was me telling you to calm down before I opened the door. But you didn't.

Love was broken ribs and jeans in July. Because bruises of that magnitude cannot be covered by shorts.

Love was yet another child conceived. Love was making me believe that you wanted me to be the mother.

Love was a rock at the top of a hill. Love was throwing away that rock when you put your hands on me again.

Love was that girl, the one that wanted to play kickball. Love was her by my side through it all.

Love was without judgement. Love was long phone calls on my porch while he was out checking on his baby's mom.

Love was wine tastings at wineries in the country, and later having that very same bottle thrown into my stomach for not wanting you to leave with my car and my credit card to see your baby mama that you lied about talking to.

Love was having the cops called after pulling me down the street by my hair, smashing your front in the display of a store front. Love was saying that everything was okay and you never touched me. Love was lifting me into your arms against the brick wall of the ally and kissing me like crazy, thanking me for not sending you to jail.

Love was the threat of burning our apartment down if I ever said a word.

Love was experience. Love was imaginary. Love forgot that I was there, but she didn't.

Love is best friends.

Love is family.

Love fucking sucks.

Love was being dragged from that girls wedding reception down a hotel hallway by the hair, back into our room, hands on throat, screams in the air, suffocated by lashes of fists to the mouth.

Love was remembering him saying "oh my god, what did I do?"

Love was Dixie cups full to the brim with water, trying to swish the blood from my mouth, hearing the words "I'm sorry" whispered into my ear and those same hands, pulling the hair away from my blood stained face.

Love was a note in the morning. Love was going to breakfast with my father, covering my face, lying about falling asleep early from too many drinks. I only had three.

Love was leaving. Love was moving home to escape the pain.

Love was going back, even after talking to the baby's mom. Love was her asking me to be there when the child was born when he had never asked.

Love was everything being said, relayed to the girl who wanted once, just to play kickball.

Love was advice. Love was support.

Love was back to hanging out in hotel rooms because family didn't accept him.

Love was family knowing what His hands could do. And his sperm count.

Love was a baby, never made to first term.

Love was him, choosing one life over the other.

Love was fake.

Love was leaving, and hours later having a replacement.

Love was stalking Facebook statuses of new love affairs.

Love was hate.

Love is overcoming. Love is patience. Love is kind.

Love is Valentine's Day. Love is hands that don't hurt, lips that don't taste, and feelings, that don't feel.

Love is alone, but still having someone, to rely on.

Love is being afraid to tell the truth, but still wanting to.

Love is relative. Love is love.

Mom's House
by Kerry Trautman

I stopped at Mom's to feed
her cat while she

was on a trip.
She left a lamp

on, three bowls of water,
and Fox News on a

staticky radio for loneliness.
Washing my hands

in the bathroom, it was dreamlike
that this once had been my daily sink.

My small, bare toes
on this tiled floor. The floors were cold

in winter. Cold the way LA sinks itself
each night into its asphalt

secret. In some cold middle of ocean there is
an undulating island of plastic garbage bits,

because nothing is ever really thrown
away. The cat slept in a warm

spot by the furnace closet, woke
suddenly to bite and lick

a hind leg. These ceilings used to hover
over my sleep. I have

read that volcano ash clouds can
drift and linger, darkening, and

even cooling atmospheres

thousands of miles away. The kitchen ceiling

has been replaced, and its skylights—
no longer leaking—clean glass, views of what's

blue. I turned the radio
dial to a top-40

station. The cat kept on licking itself,
kept nipping at what itches.

Spring is a Shaggy Green Puppy
by Mary Turzillo

Spring is a shaggy green puppy,
licking your toes in the exuberant lawn.

Spring is air-wafted pleasure
puffed out in cumulus yum,
heady as mist-fairies,
from the hide-in-sight black locust,
billowing cascades of flowers,
hiding in forest canopy, exhaling perfume.

Spring is the ultraviolet shrub,
inflorescent carousels of petals,
flattening umbels to moon-bathe.

Spring's howdy is the night I first saw you,
frisky, beard like a soft flame, oh you,
oh me, thrilled with lust for your forget-me-not eyes.

Spring's first day is when Mercury,
our mutual ruler,
pussy-foots above the horizon
after the last snow in April.

Spring is Shakespeare's birthday,
because all great poets,
including you and me,
are born in spring,
or if they aren't (why be chained to dull fact?),
they marry the first day it stops freezing,

then frisk in wet lawn like green puppies,
celebrating spring spring spring!
Oh you, let us roll in the grass,
inflamed by black locust, ruled by Mercury,
my fingers stroking your beard,
your gaze locked on my lust-gladdened eyes.

The Avenging Angels
by D.R. Wagner

We had just made our way past the barricades
When we noticed the edge of the pavement,
From the century old cut marble curbs to almost
A third of the way into the traffic lanes were filled
With blood. "That's blood," said Ramon.
"They must just have opened fire on the people
Involved with the march for human dignity that the villages
Had organized. Prepare yourselves," he said as we moved
Toward the city center. "We are the ones who have been
Sent to redeem these people." I hoped we would never
Have to do this. We are once again the avenging angels.
Our wings seemed metallic in the sweep of klieg lights
That began to sweep the park. We donned darkness
Through our skin and began to rise into the air in total silence.

Get Stuffed
by Scott Wannberg

You get stuff
to make you invulnerable,
around ten at night.
The sky looks crooked
under the harsh light
the kids made for you
so you could finally
see yourself
running scared
as the nation's sweat
turns into an ocean
only a stoical navigator as yourself
could access.

You get stuff to ward off
suffering,
and this suffering retardant
comes in a money back guaranteed tube
that's blessed by all the
major religions.
Perhaps you encountered one of these
major religions
on the so called rapid transit,
when the sun beat down
without considering if you
brought your sun screen.

Get stuff
is what the advertising agency,
working out of the stalled Camaro
in front of my building,
incessantly chirps,
whenever I dare venture
forth.

We are nothing more than the stuff we bring home,
hoping it will

dramatically alter and
affect us.
Did you ever ride that elusive perfect wave
that only you knew for sure
lives in your brain?
The sea
agreed with you,
this
morning.

The war got held up
in traffic.

Time,
for once,
to enjoy that faint music
that may or may not
actually be
real,
yet
it never stops you
from
hearing
it.

Not Love , Exactly
by Alinda Dickinson Wasner

but more like
some stupidity
a craving
late night hunger
conjured up by cars
wheels spinning
backward left to right
across blue screen
flicker light, a seizure moment
like being seated in a train
and thinking you have begun to move
but then it's just the engine on the next track over
your good luck penny
still balanced on the rail beneath you
the one you
hope to find on the return trip
perfect and gleaming
no trace of what was there
on the face of it and yet
the perfect souvenir
tucked down among the stones
and when you do
you slide into your pocket
with a sense of now-forgotten glee
and only after years of forgetting
suddenly come across it
wonder
how it got to where you find it
without you having any recollection
of ever having placed it there
in the first place
and when you turn it over
to examine it more closely
it is completely blank.

Aluminum Epiphany
by Laura Grace Weldon

Spreading his fingers
over roofing samples,
hands soundless
against metal slick
as his promotional pitch
the salesman says,
*Aluminum is the mineral
Mother Nature and Father Time
use to make gems.*

His voice moves on to
warranties and prices,
though his words
send
me
journeying.

I see
archeologists of the future
find long-buried suburbs
shining with inexplicable
treasure.

They uncover houses
sided in emeralds,
beer cans transformed
into opal cylinders,
lawn chairs of topaz,
ruby cooking pots.

They brush away
the perilous dust of that age,
careful to decontaminate
before returning home
to their children
who dream of ancient people,
awe-struck

at what it must have been like
to grow up
in the heart of
such indifferent opulence.

Road Maps
by Madison Whitacre

You are driving on the interstate
You are not sure how long you have been driving
Or when you crossed the state line
But the sun has long since fallen behind you
And the stars are guiding you toward absolution

Your headlights are shining but they provide you with no light
And you now notice that the needle on your gas gauge
Is quivering
But your car is showing no signs of stopping

You remove your hands from ten and two
And the car drives on
Possessed by the person you were before
You hit the gas
Before you decided to make this journey
Into the unknown and into the abyss

And suddenly it is dawn and you smell honey suckle
The road side is yellow and your lungs are burning
This is your life now

Before you reach the end of this road
You must first
Come to terms with scraped knees and dirty finger nails
Tears saltier than days spent by the ocean
And veins as blue as your father's eyes

You are driving on the interstate
There is no exit
But your car keeps moving forward
And the stars are guiding toward absolution
And you have miles to go
Before redemption

Motown Blues

by Rosemarie Wilson, a.k.a. One Single Rose™

My Papa was a rolling stone.
Momma found out what's going on when money got tight
then Heaven sent truth from above.
Ma heard it through the grapevine
that daddy's been playing hooky from work
out all night long
on cloud nine
dancing in the street with some two-bit super freak.
It's a shame!
Daddy was supposed to be momma's endless love,
the sunshine of her life.
It just makes me want to holler!
I thought there was nothing like the real thing,
but it was just my imagination running away with me.
Love is superstition,
signed, sealed and delivered
on the tears of a clown.
Now momma's uptight
humming inner city blues,
upset she married a Playboy
who keeps her hanging on.
Life as she knew it is now upside down on a love hangover.
What becomes of the brokenhearted, though?
Ooh, baby, baby,
in this case,
war.
The hunter gets captured by the game.
Momma loaded our shotgun—
her fingertips hot on the trigger,
sights on Daddy.
In a ball of confusion
she screamed "There's nowhere to run.
I'm leaving here.
You've really got a hold on me
but I'm going to keep on trucking, baby!
Now it's time I shop around.
Neither one of us wants to be the first to say goodbye,

but sugar pie honey bunch
I can't help myself.
Dear God,
I just wish it would rain!
Release this old heart of mine before it sinks in that man's quicksand."
I second that emotion, Ma.
Please stop in the name of love before you break my heart.
My whole world ended the moment you left me.
You're a brick house,
my girl,
three times a lady—
more than she'll ever be.
Somebody's watching me
watch out for you.
Reach out.
Come to me.
I'll cruise your heartache to higher ground
'cause ain't no mountain high enough....
Smiling faces sometimes don't tell the truth.
Daddy's was really saying something, Ma.
So, look,
I'm coming out, too!
Pops can't ever be my guy again.
I'm for real!
You deserve better.
I want you back, momma.
Come and get these memories.
Lock them away.
Throw away the key.
It's time to move on.
I pray you never have to sing the same old song again.
Please, please just don't leave me this way.

Atlas
by Eva Xanthopoulos

I want to be your Atlas, so I can
chisel away at "alas" and grant you
relief from the weight of the world
and worry from your past.
I want to create a globe of it all to carry on my shoulders,
just for a moment. Just so you can exhale the words

"At last."

Acknowledgments

Dianne Borsenik, "In a Bar, the Basement, a Microphone, and Poets" — *Age of Aquarius: Collected Poems 1981-2016* (Crisis Chronicles Press).
Nancy Brady, "Dictionary Elles" — *Three Breaths* (Drinian Press)
William Burkholder, "Soulful Song" — *Paper Kites and Daylit Dreams* (5 Acre Press).
Christopher Alexander Gellert, "It being summer" — *FORTH*.
Mindi Kirchner-Greenway, "In Medias Res" — *Song of the Rest of Us* (The Kent State University Press).
Jill Lange, "Four Skunks" — *Tributaries, A Journal of Nature Writing*.
Lennart Lundh, "Vocabulary Lesson" — *Hitchhikers in Mississippi, 1936*.
Jonie McIntire, "Love Is a Carcass" — *Not All Who Are Lost Wander* (Finishing Line Press).
Steven B. Smith, "Creation Mist" — *Medusa's Kitchen*.
D.R. Wagner, "The Avenging Angels" — *Medusa's Kitchen*.
Rosemarie Wilson, "Motown Blues" — broadside (Broadside Lotus Press).

JOHN B. BURROUGHS
EDITOR / PUBLISHER / POET
JC@CRISISCHRONICLES.COM

3431 GEORGE AVENUE
PARMA, OH 44134 USA
WWW.CRISISCHRONICLES.COM
TWITTER @JESUSCRISIS
(440) 315-0426

CRISIS CHRONICLES PRESS
VITAL INDEPENDENT LITERATURE SINCE 2008
CCPRESS.BLOGSPOT.COM   FACEBOOK.COM/CRISISCHRONICLESPRESS

www.ingramcontent.com/pod-product-compliance
Lightning Source LLC
Chambersburg PA
CBHW071211160426
43196CB00011B/2256